For William T. Hornaday and all those
who dream of following in his pioneering
footsteps—passionate protectors of
wildlife and wild lands

—K.W.Z.

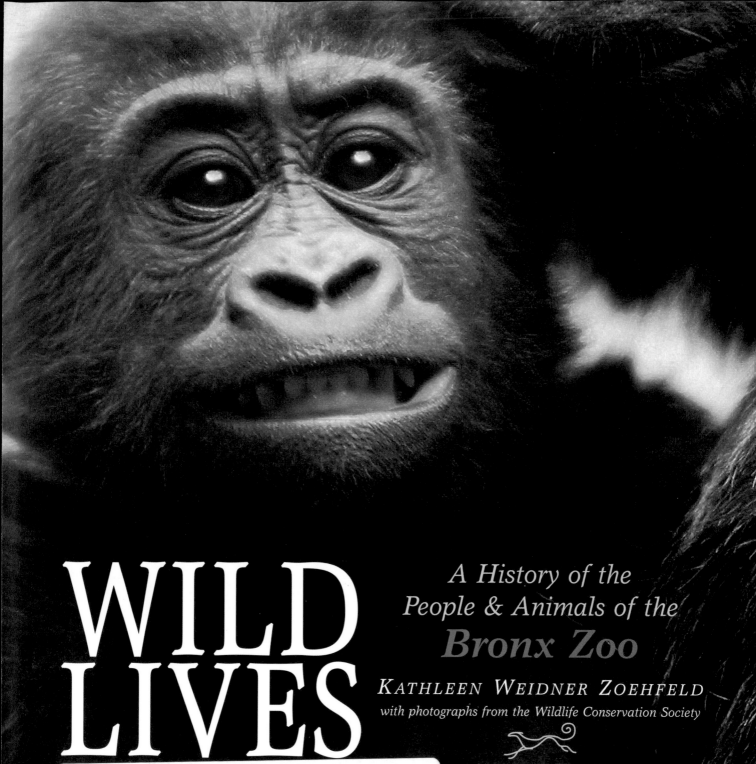

WILD LIVES

A History of the People & Animals of the
Bronx Zoo

KATHLEEN WEIDNER ZOEHFELD

with photographs from the Wildlife Conservation Society

ALFRED A. KNOPF
New York

RING-TAILED
LEMUR

The beauty and genius of a work of art may be reconceived, though its first material expression be destroyed; a vanished harmony may yet again inspire the composer; but when the last individual of a race of living beings breathes no more, another heaven and another earth must pass before such a one can be again.

—William Beebe, *The Bird*

BARINGO
GIRAFFE

CONTENTS

ZOO AWAKENING

On a cold, rainy afternoon in November 1899, Director William T. Hornaday flung open the wrought-iron gates of the Bronx Zoo for the first time. Horse-drawn carriages had arrived, carrying important people from all over the city. The drivers parked outside the gates, and the excited guests stepped out. Women in their long skirts and fancy hats, men in dark suits and derby caps rushed in and gathered for the opening ceremonies. The speeches were brief, and the crowds were soon staring in wonder at the bears in their new dens and pressing to get a look at the buffalo, elk, and caribou in their pens. Boys in knee pants and woolen socks hurried to see the storks and pelicans

The Bronx Zoo opened its doors for the first time on November 8, 1899.

1

Zoo-goers crowd around the bear dens on Opening Day.

BROWN PELICAN

in the Aquatic Birds' House. Girls in short, frilly dresses gasped at the alligator and python in the Reptile House. Never had the visitors seen so many strange and fascinating creatures in one place.

As the years went by, New York City grew—its skyscrapers blocking out forest and sky, the din of its trains and "horseless carriages" drowning out the songs of birds. New Yorkers came to consider the Zoo, up in the rural, woodsy Bronx, a pleasant diversion from the pressures of city life. Although zoo-goers enjoyed the excitement of seeing unfamiliar or exotic animals, few inquired about the habitats those animals came from or what their lives in the wild might have been like. Most people

William T. Hornaday, first director of the Bronx Zoo, at his desk.

2

regarded animals as objects to be captured and tamed, or to be hunted and killed for pleasure or profit. They regarded wild habitats as places to be subdued or "developed" for human uses. Unless an animal seemed truly abused and miserable in its cage, zoo-goers rarely questioned whether the confinement of animals could be justified solely for the sake of human pleasure and entertainment.

But William T. Hornaday wanted that to change. From the very start, he envisioned a new kind of zoo: a zoo that would both entertain and educate, a zoo that would help change people's indifferent or destructive attitudes toward wild animals.

Today people know that many wild animal species are threatened with extinction and that their wild habitats are rapidly disappearing. One hundred years ago, Hornaday and a few visionary people like him were among the first to recognize that wildlife was in grave danger. He and the Bronx Zoo's founders took the first steps to protect wildlife. And they hoped to create a zoo that would give zoo-goers a deeper respect for the animals and a greater understanding of their lives in the wild.

In 1896, before laying out the plans for the Zoo, Hornaday traveled around Europe,

"What would happen . . . if Noah should arrive with his arkful of animals and turn them loose."

studying what the older zoos had done right and thinking about what things could be improved. The average European zoo of the day was only about thirty acres (approximately the size of fourteen city blocks), and the limited space meant that their animals were very closely confined. Hornaday and the founders of the Bronx Zoo believed this was detrimental to the animals. And they saw that the cramped, unnatural cages prevented people from learning about and appreciating the animals as wild creatures in their own right. In their *Preliminary Plan*, the founders announced that they would create a zoo where "the living creatures can be kept under conditions most closely approximating those with which nature usually surrounds them, in spaces so extensive that with many species the sense of confinement is either lost or greatly diminished, yet at the same time sufficiently limited that the animals are not inaccessible or invisible to the visitor."

AMERICAN ALLIGATOR

A visitor observes a snow leopard within an iron cage inside the Lion House, February 1906.

The city government agreed to provide a large parcel of public land where the new zoological park could be developed. Hornaday spent three weeks studying the city's parklands. When he finally arrived at South Bronx Park, he was elated. Here were 261 acres of rolling meadows and lush woodlands, bordered by lakes to the north and by the Bronx River to the east. He explored every nook and cranny of the park, all the time imagining "what would happen . . . if Noah should arrive with his arkful of animals and turn them

The Elephant House was an example of the Zoo's ornate architecture. It opened in 1908.

Hornaday struggled to achieve a balance between the animals' need to be free and the need of zoo-goers to actually see the animals. This became an ongoing dilemma, in which the early ideal of giving animals extensive spaces was often sacrificed. Throughout the early 1900s at the Bronx Zoo—more properly known as the New York Zoological Park—it was not uncommon to see animals locked up in iron cages or in small pens. People went to the

loose." The landscape was perfect for the new zoo, and Hornaday was determined to preserve the natural beauty of the park, incorporating the trees and hills and rocky outcrops in the animals' enclosures. The founders, as well, declared that no trees should be cut down in the building of the Zoo. However, special dispensation was given to the beavers, "who shall be allowed to cut down several small trees that stand in the bog where it is proposed the Beaver Pond shall be located."

Like many of the animals, the beavers did not entirely cooperate with plans, and it was "on account of the annoyance and disappointment to visitors caused by the persistence of the beavers . . . in keeping out of sight" that Hornaday finally gave in to pressure and put a beaver on display in the Small Mammal House.

In modern exhibits, such as the World of Birds rain forest, observers may not see the animals immediately—it can take time to spot them, just as it would in the wild.

"**People must understand the natural world in order to save it, and themselves.**"

Zoo to watch the lion in its elegant prison, the elephant chained to a bald patch of ground, or the hippopotamus, out of water and behind bars, in a grand architectural setting.

After decades of gradual improvements, the world's best zoos today have achieved Hornaday's early dream of giving animals plenty of space and showing them in their natural surroundings. But many people question whether anyone can justify keeping animals in a zoo of any kind. Given the abundance of good nature documentaries on television, they wonder whether anyone needs to visit a zoo to learn about wildlife anymore. Are even the roomiest, best-run zoos unfair to animals? Should zoos close and shift all their efforts to preserving animals in the wild? Hornaday would undoubtedly answer, no! Zoos are still the best way for urban and suburban dwellers to learn about their wild heritage. Nevertheless, all good zoo directors must keep these questions in mind.

In the twenty-first century, more than 2 million people will visit the Bronx Zoo every year. Like our great-great-grandparents, we still go, for the most part, to have fun—to explore the wooded coves and rocky crannies and thrill over the exotic animals, to drink our sodas and devour our French fries and soft pretzels. But as we experience the Bronx Zoo's exhibits, we also have the opportunity to learn about the lives of the animals and about the wild habitats they come from. In modern exhibits, it often takes time and patience to spot the animals, much as it would if you were hiking in the wild: Wolf cubs curl up to sleep in the fallen leaves of their forest glen. Crocodiles float as still as logs in their tropical river. Cheetahs crouch under thick bushes, letting their spotted coats blend in with the dappled light and shadow. The animals are no longer on display for the convenience of zoogoers, as they were in 1899. To *really* get to know the animals, you have to move into their world—at least for a moment.

Good zoos bring a bit of the living wilderness inside the walls of our cities and call us to pay attention to the natural world. Looking into the eyes of a gorilla, smelling the fishy breath of a sea lion, or feeling the earthshaking trumpet of an elephant may spark an understanding of our interconnectedness with nature and the wilderness—perhaps more memorably than anything on a cold television screen ever could. And as William G. Conway, director of the Zoo from 1961 through 1999, said: "People must understand

6

the natural world in order to save it, and themselves."

Throughout the more than one hundred years since the Zoo's opening day, the people of the Bronx Zoo have tried to carry on the pioneering ideals of its founders: They have developed better and better ways to care for the Zoo's animals, to educate people, and to inspire them to preserve the world's endangered animals and wild places. But it was not an easy path! How did the Bronx Zoo of opening day in 1899 evolve to become the Bronx Zoo we know today? All the goals were set in place right from the start, but the understanding of those goals has changed over the decades—changes led by the innovative work of the Bronx Zoo's scientists and driven by the needs of the animals, both at the Zoo and in the wild.

SAVING THE GREAT AMERICAN BISON

William T. Hornaday was born in Indiana in 1854. When he was three years old, his family loaded up their horse-drawn wagon and, with a flock of poultry in tow and livestock following behind, made their way to a new farm on the Des Moines River in Iowa. "Billy" grew up there, the youngest of seven children. His farm chores were light, and he was free to roam the wild prairie near his home. Often he'd hunt for pheasants, ducks, and squirrels for his family's supper. But it was on the prairie that his deep appreciation of wildlife began. Even as a child, he said, he felt that it was wrong to kill harmless creatures simply for sport. He resolved to kill only what his family needed.

Sadly, William was orphaned at the age of fifteen, but with the help of generous relatives, he soon went off to college, where he began to study natural history. He taught himself the art of taxidermy—the skinning, preparing, and stuffing of animals for display. One of his jobs in college was to mount a collection of native animals for the college museum. Although taxidermy involved the killing of animals, it was considered a necessity for scientific studies, and William felt he had found his career. After finishing his sophomore year at Iowa State

William Hornaday on expedition as a young man.

University, he went to work for one of the foremost taxidermists in the country—the Natural Science Establishment of Henry Augustus Ward. There he prepared animals to be exhibited in the finest museums in the country. In his early twenties, as an employee of Ward, he explored the jungles of India, Ceylon, the Malay Peninsula, and Borneo. With the animals he brought home, he put together the most varied and colorful collection of museum specimens ever made by one man up until that time.

Having earned a great reputation as a field naturalist and taxidermist, Hornaday was offered the position of chief taxidermist at the Smithsonian Institution's National Museum in Washington, D.C. He worked hard in his new position, learning newer and better methods of stuffing and preparing wild animals for exhibit and creating some of the most highly praised

museum displays in the world. But as much as collecting and preserving wild animals interested Hornaday, it was not satisfying him. So in 1888, the Smithsonian appointed him the chief curator of their Department of Living Animals. All the museum's taxidermists went to this department when they needed to observe live animals and get ideas for posing and arranging their exhibits.

Hornaday encouraged the museum directors to open the living collection to the public. Washingtonians and tourists visiting the nation's capital seemed eager to see the herds of deer and the foxes, lynx, eagles, and other animals that Hornaday collected out west. Once the museum directors saw how popular the live exhibits were, Hornaday pushed further and helped convince them and the U.S. Congress that "a nation so far in advance in the

AMERICAN BALD EAGLE

march of progress as the United States" should have a zoological park under the federal government's protection.

Hornaday designed the National Zoo, which opened in Washington, D.C., in 1891 and has gone on to flourish as one of the world's great zoos. One of Hornaday's goals for the nation's zoo was to offer a refuge so that "native animals . . . threatened with extinction might live and perpetuate their species in peace." No zoo in the world had ever expressed such a goal. But in its formative years, the National Zoo's development was hampered by disagreements between its founders and the political leaders of the day. After a year of trying to get his creative new ideas under way, Hornaday found he was receiving no political support—in fact, his idea of the zoo as a wildlife refuge would be shelved for decades—and he quit in 1890,

CANADIAN LYNX

Theodore Roosevelt in 1885, outfitted with a deerskin hunting suit and a rifle. Roosevelt helped found the Boone and Crockett Club.

William T. Hornaday, director of the Zoo from 1899 to 1926.

several months before the grand opening. Dispirited and disillusioned, he moved to Buffalo, New York, to supervise a large real estate corporation.

Meanwhile, a group of prominent New Yorkers was busy forming the New York Zoological Society, or NYZS. Most of the Society's promoters were serious big-game hunters who, in 1887, had created the famous Boone and Crockett Club. Headed by Theodore Roosevelt, then an important political leader in New York (and later president of the United States from 1901 to 1909), the club's main purpose was to speak out against unsportsmanlike hunting practices—such as the killing of animals for sale and profit, wasteful hunting, or hunting with an unfair or improper advantage over the animals—which were leaving vast numbers of game animals dead and threatening whole species with extinction. Where other groups had failed, the Boone and Crockett Club activists soon earned the support of the New York State government, and the New York Zoological Society was born. Members of the NYZS were put in charge of the foundation of what would be—at the cusp of the new century—the largest, most innovative zoo in the world.

Although Hornaday had left the field, his reputation as a zoo designer was remembered. In 1896, the NYZS asked Hornaday to take over as director of the soon-to-be-created New York Zoological Park. He had turned down a similar offer from the city of Pittsburgh just six months earlier because, after his disappointment in Washington, he felt that his "ambition in that direction had died, past all possibility of resurrection." But the NYZS's plan for the new zoo was unique. Reading it, Hornaday found himself filled to the brim with ideas about its many "magnificent possibilities." He accepted the Society's offer.

The first few years kept him busy—buildings

had to be designed and built, and animals had to be obtained from many far-off corners of the Earth. But as soon as the practical details of getting the new Zoological Park operating smoothly were worked out, Hornaday and his NYZS colleagues resolved that they would make the preservation and protection of American wildlife one of the Bronx Zoo's top priorities. In a characteristically dramatic statement, Hornaday declared, "Throughout the entire continent of North America, nearly every wild quadruped, bird, reptile, and fish is marked for destruction."

If Hornaday was passionate, it's because he had learned the gruesome facts through first-hand experience while at the Smithsonian. Back in 1883, while he was still the top taxidermist there, he had read a magazine article that troubled him deeply. In the western United States, it said, the American bison, more commonly known as buffalo, were on the verge of extinction. Some naturalists were predicting that the buffalo would be gone within a decade.

Before Europeans arrived in the 1600s, about 75 million buffalo roamed the prairies of America in vast herds. As late as 1870, there were still between 40 and 50 million. By 1883—a mere thirteen years later—buffalo had nearly vanished off the face of the Earth.

Hornaday had long detested the way the buffalo were pursued and slaughtered by hunters and sportsmen. Sometimes sportsmen made a game of seeing how many they could kill from

Buffalo were abundant in America before Europeans arrived, but by 1883 there were very few left.

a train car; hunters sometimes killed them just for their hides, or for their tongues or the meat of their humps, which were considered delicacies. Many were killed to deprive Native Americans of their food and livelihood. The plains of the American West were littered with the skulls and bones of dead and discarded buffalo.

The facts hit Hornaday hard. He searched the National Museum to see how many good buffalo specimens they had. He found one—only one—not very well-preserved buffalo and a couple of mounted heads. He persuaded the director of the museum to allow him to plan an expedition to Montana, where he hoped to find a few healthy specimens that he could preserve for all time.

Traveling by train, he took his crew to Miles City, a remote prairie town where a few scat-

A buffalo hide yard in Dodge City, Kansas, 1878. Buffalo were often killed for their hides, their tongues, or the meat in their humps.

tered buffalo had recently been sighted. When he got there, the local people told him that all of them had been killed.

Hornaday was packing up to return home empty-handed when he ran into a rancher who said he knew of a small herd that occasionally wandered through his land. The rancher was happy to direct Hornaday and his crew to his ranch north of town. With a six-mule wagon and horses supplied by the local Army post, Hornaday and his crew carried their supplies to the ranch and set up camp on Little Dry Creek. After only two days, they were able to

capture and kill two old buffalo bulls.

Unfortunately, Hornaday had come late in the spring, and the animals were already beginning to shed their winter coats. They were too tattered and scruffy to be good museum specimens. He decided to return to the ranch outside of Miles City the next fall, when the buffalo's coats would be heavy and thick again in readiness for the cold winter. Before he left, he begged the local cowboys and hunters not to kill the buffalo. Hornaday was persuasive— none of them killed any that summer.

The next September, Hornaday returned to

the ranch and set up a base camp a few miles farther west, on the bank of Big Porcupine Creek. He and his men were able to collect several good specimens for the museum. Once back in Washington, Hornaday prepared six of those animals for a huge diorama. The dramatic display was unique for its time. Chicago's Field Museum and the American Museum of Natural History in New York had been experi- menting with new dioramas that showed ani- mals with paintings of their habitats behind them. But Hornaday's buffalo display was the first large family grouping of wild animals— male and female, young and old—posed natu- rally, and artistically arranged with bones, soil, plants, fossils, and other specimens from their natural environment. The exhibit stood in the Smithsonian from 1887 until 1955, when

Hornaday's dramatic buffalo exhibit opened at the Smithsonian in 1887.

museum workers dismantled it to be shipped to Montana, where it remained in storage until 1996. Today the restored exhibit can be seen at the Museum of the Northern Great Plains in Fort Benton, Montana.

Hornaday's buffalo exhibit was so popular, it changed the basic philosophy of natural history museums all over the world. The old, traditional displays—single animals scientifically labeled and mounted individually on stark pedestals—gave way to the vastly more popular habitat groups. Thanks to Hornaday's innovation, natural history museums were being transformed from scientific storehouses for animals sorted according to genus or species into institutions of public education, which sought to provide adults and children with a deeper understanding not only of different species but of their distant wild habitats as well.

In spite of the great success of his exhibit, Hornaday expressed shame at his own killing of so many buffalo. Perhaps even then he was feeling pangs of guilt about using his expert taxidermy skills as the only means of preserving wildlife. But back in 1887, Hornaday simply could not believe there was any hope the buffalo might survive. The forces against them seemed too great. Stuffed buffalo inside a glass display case might soon be the only buffalo the children of the world and their children's children would ever get to see.

By 1899, Hornaday's new position at the Bronx Zoo had restored his hope and rekindled his creativity and determination. Soon he was one of the foremost experts in the country working to ensure that the great American bison would survive—alive—forever. His first step was to establish a small but hardy herd at the Zoo.

Very few people of the time understood that if they kept up their wasteful hunting and their exploitation of wildlife, entire species would

> "Throughout the entire continent of North America, nearly every wild quadruped, bird, reptile, and fish is marked for destruction."

become extinct. In fact, many species, such as the passenger pigeon, had already been annihilated. Hornaday knew that the majestic buffalo would be next. The total number of buffalo in North America (in the wild and in captivity combined) had dwindled to less than 1,000. The United States government was trying to manage the one remaining wild herd—a straggly little group of fewer than twenty-five—in Yellowstone National Park. Hornaday worried that the Yellowstone herd was too small and too closely confined to perpetuate itself successfully.

15

In 1907, Hornaday arranged to have fifteen healthy Bronx Zoo buffalo shipped to the Wichita Bison Preserve.

The buffalo were transported from a nearby rail yard to Grand Central Station, then on to Cache, Oklahoma, in two forty-four-foot-long rail cars.

In Oklahoma, the buffalo were loaded onto horse-drawn carts, which carried them the rest of the way to the preserve.

In 1905, he wrote to the U.S. Secretary of Agriculture, James Wilson, and recommended that the government establish a protected herd within the Wichita Forest Reserve in Oklahoma. He promised to provide healthy buffalo from the Bronx Zoo and ship them safely to the reserve. By 1907, Wilson and Hornaday had convinced the U.S. Congress to allocate money for a Wichita Bison Preserve, and it was soon properly fenced and made ready for its new inhabitants.

Fifteen Bronx Zoo buffalo were carted to a nearby train yard, coaxed onto two forty-four-foot-long train cars (along with plenty of hay and water!), and transported down to Grand Central Station and then out across the 1,800 rail miles to the little town of Cache, Oklahoma. There, they disembarked from their train cars and were loaded again into horse-drawn carts, which carried them the remaining fourteen miles from the railroad stop to the preserve. It was a huge event. People all along the route came out to cheer the buffalo on their way to their new home.

The Bronx Zoo continued to supply buffalo to government-protected herds in Oklahoma and other parts of the West for seven years. In fact, the Bronx Zoo provided the first animals for four of the ten major public herds in the nation. Thanks to the efforts of Hornaday and the NYZS, we are still able to see living buffalo. Today over 100,000 buffalo live in

Many buffalo like these were relocated to the wild from the Bronx Zoo, joining government-protected herds in different parts of the West.

Bird of paradise skins. When bird feathers on hats became a fashion craze, many exotic birds were killed to meet the demand.

protected ranges across the country.

Throughout the rest of his time as director of the Zoo, there was hardly a conservation issue in which Hornaday was not involved. He took a leading role in saving the fur seals of the Pribilof Islands from fur hunters. He fought for strict hunting laws. He worked for legislation to prevent the sale of wild game for profit. And when hats decorated with feathers (and even entire stuffed birds!) became a fashion craze, he campaigned against the frivolous sale of wild birds for their feathers and skins.

Although Hornaday maintained the opinion—very common among farmers and hunters (and just about everyone else) at the time—that predatory animals such as wolves and mountain lions were "murderous vermin," and although he cared little about *their* preservation, his ideas about wildlife conservation were revolutionary. The New York Zoological Society became the nation's leader in conservation efforts during his tenure. Our ideas about conservation have evolved over the decades, but Hornaday was among the first to speak out for wildlife. His clear, passionate voice awakened zoo-goers and people all across the nation to the tragic loss of wild species that was happening right before their eyes. And his heroic actions helped convince people that something could be done to stop it.

Closer to home at the Zoo, however, the director's ideas about educating zoo-goers and keeping animals comfortable and healthy had, by modern standards, a long way to go.

THE FIRST ANIMALS ARRIVE!

The summer of 1899—with opening day looming just a few months away—was a wild one for Director Hornaday. Unfortunately, it was not wild in any of the ways he might have wished. There would be no time for thinking about country-wide conservation policies that summer. He had his hands full at home, supervising the completion of the first major zoo buildings. Construction was going slowly, and curious New Yorkers wandered in by the dozens to stand around and watch and, more often than not, to get in the way. To make matters worse, while most of the animals' dens and cages were not yet finished and many of the people who would be taking care of the animals were still not hired, animals had begun arriving from far and near!

Hornaday hoped that the first animal to arrive at the Zoo would be a healthy young grizzly bear. He planned to line up a professional photographer to document the historic event. Unfortunately, a grizzly bear proved harder to come by than Hornaday had anticipated. Instead of a bear, the Zoo's first animals were a pair of bedraggled white-tailed prairie dogs from Wyoming. He called off the photography session, and the sickly little prairie dogs were tended to and eventually transferred to their new Prairie Dog Village.

After the prairie dogs, new animals began arriving every day—local animals such as the star-nosed mole, opossum, skunk, weasel, flying squirrel, and raccoon, and unusual, harder-to-keep animals from more far-flung places, including a giant Venezuelan anteater, three orangutans, a Bengal tiger, two polar bears, a woodland caribou, nine American elk, six pronghorn antelopes, and four California sea lions.

The flood of animals had begun, but the ark was far from ready! That summer, temporary animal sheds and fenced enclosures had to be set up in the middle of the park. Florida otters were squeezed into the empty turtle tanks, pythons were held in cardboard boxes, and the unhappy polar bears rubbed the fur off their backs on the rocks of their temporary den. The young orangutans, who needed special attention, had to be moved into Hornaday's house, where his wife, Josephine Hornaday, watched over them, desperately trying to help them through various stomach upsets by feeding them boiled rice with milk and ripe bananas. Many animals died from inadequate food and

The very first animals to arrive at the Bronx Zoo were a pair of sickly prairie dogs. Today the Zoo's prairie dogs, such as this one, are flourishing.

FLYING SQUIRREL

quarters, and years afterward the practical as well as compassionate Hornaday expressed how deeply he regretted getting many of the Zoo's animals before their dens and cages had been adequately prepared.

By the autumn of 1899, Hornaday had finally hired two brilliant young men to help him with the new animals and to train and oversee a staff of animal keepers. Hornaday and the members of the New York Zoological Society had agreed ahead of time that they wanted their department heads to be different from the usual rough-and-tumble animal managers who acted as head keepers at most zoos of the time. Rather than being mere keepers, their managers would be true curators—people with scientific training who would be able to study their animals' needs, collect accurate data, and develop the best possible conditions.

RACCOON

Hornaday chose Raymond L. Ditmars, a feisty twenty-three-year-old newspaper reporter, to become assistant curator of reptiles. In his spare time Ditmars had founded the Harlem Zoological Society. His first job had been to work as an assistant in the Insect Hall at the American Museum of Natural History, and during that time he had also built an impressive private collection of native American snakes.

When the overworked Hornaday was having trouble deciding on a good candidate for assistant curator of birds, one of the most prominent members of the NYZS, Henry Fairfield Osborn—also the director of vertebrate paleontology at the American Museum of Natural History and an esteemed professor of zoology at Columbia University—recommended one of his most outstanding students, twenty-two-year-old C. William Beebe. Hornaday's two new curators, Beebe and Ditmars, would shape the future of the Zoo in powerful and compelling ways.

For now, things were beginning to fall into

In the Zoo's earliest days, Josephine Hornaday looked after orangutans; today they are thriving.

When a python refused to eat, Ditmars and his crew tried to stuff dead rabbits and pigeons down its throat with a pole.

place—buildings were completed, curators were hired, and new animals continued to arrive. But despite the combined intelligence and determined efforts of the humans, some of the animals were refusing to settle in and, as Hornaday would put it, "act rationally." When one of the twenty-foot pythons lost interest in his food, Ditmars and his crew tried tying dead rabbits and pigeons together with string and forcing them down the serpent's throat with a long pole. The black-tailed jackrabbits, who developed the disconcerting habit of flinging themselves into their fence and breaking their necks anytime a visitor approached, were an inscrutable problem.

When the first few American bison arrived from ranches in Texas and Oklahoma, Hornaday relished putting them out on their new range, which offered, according to Hornaday, "everything that buffalo could possibly desire in this world." But the buffalo suffered from gas from the lush New York grass—a much richer diet than they were used to on the prairie. Even worse, the pronghorn antelopes, which had arrived a bit earlier, were dying off one after the other. No one could figure out why. The food that was offered and the New York climate were not suitable for the pronghorns, but at that time no one knew what a healthy

Buffalo from Texas and Oklahoma arrived at the Zoo and were placed on their new range.

pronghorn diet and environment might be.

The Bronx Zoo was not the first zoo in the United States—far from it. Besides the National Zoo in Washington, D.C., more than twenty U.S. cities had created zoos since the end of the Civil War in 1865. But even in the relatively spacious National Zoo, some animals became lethargic in their cages. Other animals became frantic. Unnatural behaviors and sudden unexplainable deaths were common among zoo animals everywhere. Many wild animals did not even make it to their intended zoos—an appalling number died at the hands of professional animal dealers in the process of capture and shipment.

In the opinion of most zookeepers of 1900, Hornaday included, wild animals caught and forced into captivity needed to be mastered and made to behave. When the animals themselves seemed uninterested in cooperating, a bit of human force might be applied, with the idea that it was for the animal's own good. Today these ideas about animal care might seem funny to us, or even cruel. The problem, for the most part, was not lack of intelligence or compassion, but lack of knowledge. When it sense methods often had no positive results. Hornaday and his staff had to begin letting go of their preconceptions and start trying new things. Force-feeding pythons was not one of their better ideas. But Hornaday and his new curators were scientists. In defiance of the attitudes held by most other zookeepers of the time, Hornaday determined that the unnatural behaviors, sickness, and death so common among captive animals could no longer be seen as simply an acceptable part of the zookeeping process. He and his curators were determined to find out why some species thrived and others didn't. They were dedicated to the well-being of the animals under their care, and like all good scientists they developed and tried out new ideas, made careful observations, and learned from their mistakes.

By 1901, the Bronx Zoo had a small permanent staff of veterinarians. It is difficult for us to imagine today, but though humans had been keeping zoos for centuries, the Bronx Zoo's Medical Department and its Animal Hospital, built in 1916 and run by Dr. W. Reid Blair, was the first veterinary establishment at any zoo in the world. The Zoo's founders were very proud of it. For the first time, staff veterinarians were able to give close scientific attention to understanding many of the diseases and discomforts that plagued animals in captivity. Many of the ideas about animal care we take for granted today were learned, step by step, at the Bronx Zoo. In part because of the work of Bronx Zoo

Dr. W. Reid Blair (left), a staff veterinarian, and Director Hornaday operate on a bear.

came to the lesser-known animals, Hornaday believed that where actual knowledge was lacking, common sense might be effectively applied. If wholesome food was offered, the animals should eat and thrive, because that's what made sense. But when animals refused to eat or became glum and sickly, the common

The Reptile House, Rodent Collection. Animals were often displayed in rows of labeled cages.

scientists, we know that animals need the types of foods they find in their natural environments. Most need a feeling of space and freedom. Many need the opportunity to play and to forage or hunt for their food.

Hornaday and the Zoo's founders tried hard to stick to their early goal of transforming the common concept of a "zoo" into that of a "wildlife preserve," where animals could live in conditions as close to their natural surroundings as possible. The larger North American animals, in particular, they hoped to show "not in paddocks but in the free range of large enclosures, in which the forests, rocks, and natural features of the landscape will give people an impression of the life, habits, and native surroundings of these different types." And with many of the large North American animals, the Zoo did fairly well.

Unfortunately, the Zoo's new Reptile and Lion houses, the Elephant House, and the Antelope House were all designed to resemble the traditional zoo buildings of Europe—architecturally grand but devoid of all indications of the wild habitats from which the animals came. Looking back at the Zoo from today's perspective, we'd say the innovative goal of creating "natural surroundings" was still far from being met. The old-fashioned principles prevailed, and most of the animals were displayed in sterile cages, row upon row, grouped by species and labeled, with little or no information on where the animal had come from.

While Hornaday's museum exhibits were revolutionizing natural history museums, zoos were still struggling to recognize that animals should be shown in their natural habitats.

The Bird House, designed by William Beebe, opened to the public in 1905.

And though the Bronx Zoo was the first to recognize the need, implementation proved difficult.

After the initial hurdles of opening the new zoo had been overcome, a few inroads began to be made. One of the most innovative new exhibits at the Zoological Park was the Bird House, which opened to the public in 1905. The interior of the Bird House was designed by the Zoo's new bird curator, William Beebe. The building's glass roof gave the inside an airy, outdoor look. The central attraction was a thirty-six-foot-long "flying cage," filled with dramatic plants and colorful songbirds. Never before had zoo birds been exhibited in such a spacious environment. Skeptical keepers at more old-fashioned zoos argued that the newly introduced birds would be dazed and drop dead when introduced into such a large, busy environment, and that even if a few did manage to survive, zoo-goers would be frustrated trying to find the birds among the foliage. Instead, visitors loved the new Bird House, and the birds thrived!

Beebe's cage came closest of all the early

enclosures to the NYZS's goal of showing wildlife in the "conditions with which nature surrounds them." But with most of the animals at the Zoo, the sad fact was no one knew anything about their actual lives in the wild. At that time, although a few famous big-game hunters and professional animal dealers had written books about wild animals (mostly with the intention of telling folks how to locate and capture or kill the animals), virtually no one had ventured into the field to do long-term studies of animal lives and behavior. When it came to understanding natural conditions, zookeepers were in the dark.

Using a trained staff of veterinarians was a huge innovation, but it wasn't enough. Hornaday and the directors of the NYZS realized that if the Zoo's precious animals were to survive their capture and captivity, their keepers would have to pioneer yet another new tradition: Out beyond the fences and borders of the Zoo, they would look for new ways of observing and understanding animals in their natural environments.

> Our wild creatures are not immortal; and, like human beings, they live out their allotted lives and pass away. The great majority do not perpetuate themselves in captivity, and the depleted ranks must be filled.
>
> —William T. Hornaday, *Popular Official Guide to the New York Zoological Park*

ADDING TO THE COLLECTION

Finishing up an important expedition in the autumn of 1906, Curator of Reptiles Raymond Ditmars traveled up the coast of Brazil, from São Paulo to Rio de Janeiro. Inside his suitcase, curled between the shirts and the clean underwear, was a rare crimson-and-gold-ringed snake. As the train chugged along, Ditmars scribbled in his notebook, trying to work out a suitable design for the boxes that would carry his newly acquired collection of South American snakes safely home to the Zoo. There was no such thing as airline transport in those days. The snakes would have to be kept comfortable for a long and possibly stormy steamer journey up the Atlantic from Rio to New York Harbor.

Getting any exotic animals to the Zoo alive and healthy was an ongoing problem. As he scribbled, Ditmars worried in particular about the rare fish-eating liophis in his satchel. A snake can go a long time without a meal, but he cannot go forever. In town after town along the way, Ditmars tried to find a fish or a frog that would be acceptable to his finicky companion. But drought had stricken the countryside that season. Frog ponds had dried up and freshwater fish were nowhere to be found.

Once in the big city of Rio, he hoped he'd find a market where he might buy a frog or even a few goldfish for his hungry serpent. It would be a few days before their steamer left for New York—only a few days to make sure his prize specimen would be well fed and content before it began its long journey.

28

Ditmars combed the city, but fresh fish did not seem to be available anywhere. After a long morning's search, exhausted and hungry for his own lunch, he stopped in a small park near a public fountain. As he stared into the water, he saw exactly what he needed! He dabbled his fingers in, and a group of small silvery fish swam up to investigate. These fish would be easy to catch. But Ditmars figured he had better not get caught fishing in a public fountain in Rio! There was no time to ask the police for permission—he imagined the poor snake dying of starvation by the time everyone had agreed and all the proper forms had been filled out. He waited until nightfall. When the coast was clear, he snuck up to the fountain, dipped his straw hat into the water, and scooped out several fish. He slipped them into a small tin pail he had brought along, concealed in a brown paper bag.

Back at his hotel, he filled his bathtub with water and poured the fish in. They swam around the big tub happily enough. And he counted them contentedly. Altogether he had caught just enough fish for three square meals for the snake. Poised eagerly on Ditmars's bed, the snake awaited his first meal in many days. He gulped down three fish that evening.

The next day, Ditmars was surprised to find bread crumbs floating in his bathtub with the remaining fish. He fed two more of the fish to his snake that night.

The following day, there were even more bread crumbs floating in his tub. By the time the last fish was gone, he began to notice that the chambermaid was giving him sharp looks. He pulled aside one of the bellboys who knew some English and asked him what the chambermaid thought he had done with the fish. He replied, "She thinks you ate them." Ditmars smiled to himself, thinking that the bellboy must have had his own suspicions as well.

Ditmars began his snake-collecting and police-evading career as a young boy, growing up in an apartment on the Upper West Side of Manhattan. His parents had their doubts about snakes as pets. But Raymond had his eye on a large water snake in the local pet-store window. He described it to his parents as being "a lot like a garter snake only bigger." And his parents reluctantly said yes.

He was glad they were out when he brought the snake home. It was four feet long and two inches thick, and he had quite a tussle wrangling it into its new terrarium. When his parents returned, he didn't have the courage to show them. He told them the snake was nervous and needed a rest.

What it *really* needed was a meal! Raymond ran the few blocks from home to Central Park. He crept through the grass on the shore of Harlem Meer, keeping out of sight of policemen. He caught a big green-headed frog, slipped it in his pocket, and took it home to feed his new snake. The snake gobbled up the frog and then waved its head back and forth,

CORN SNAKE

searching for something else to devour. Raymond wondered how long he could continue dodging the policemen in Central Park.

To delay his parents' actually seeing the snake, he set up a screened-in sunporch for it out on his fire escape. The next day, the police were banging on the Ditmarses' door. The neighbors—seeing the huge serpent in its light screen cage, just slithering distance from their own windows—were in an uproar. They had called the police and demanded that the beast be removed. When Raymond's father finally saw the snake, he hit the roof, and all snakes were banished from the household. Raymond shut himself in his room that night and cried. But that was the beginning, not the end, of Raymond's life with snakes.

On a special expedition to the Everglades with the insect curator at the American Museum of Natural History, where he had landed his first real job, Raymond captured king snakes, chicken snakes, and corn snakes and filled his bedroom once again.

When he was asked to work at the Zoological Park at the age of twenty-three, he was thrilled to have his large private collection of snakes accepted as the basis of the Zoo's first reptile collection. No doubt his parents were thrilled, too! He finally had his dream job—to be out in the world observing the creatures he loved the most and bringing them, not home, but to the Zoological Park, where millions of children could see them and experience them firsthand.

In its first years, most of the Bronx Zoo's animals were either donated by private collectors or ranchers or brought home from expeditions by Zoo curators like Raymond Ditmars and William Beebe. But collecting animals in the wild had its costs. At that time the majority of animals collected from wild environments died—either during capture or during shipment to the zoo. Most zoos purchased animals from professional animal dealers, who often ended up killing dozens of animals in the process of capturing one or two. For the most part, zoo professionals didn't worry about destroying habitats and countless numbers of the very animals they hoped to display—for them it was simply an inevitable part of the collecting and shipping process.

Hornaday dreamed of a time when all or most of the Zoo's new animals could be bred, born, and raised right at the Zoo. In fact, as he was designing the National Zoo in Washington, he wrote optimistically about the possibilities of captive breeding, when most other zoo directors had not yet given it a thought. But that was still a dream for the

Keeper with a regal python, 1907.

future. The stresses of captivity prevented most zoo animals from producing healthy offspring. After the Zoo's opening years, generous donations from private collectors began to taper off. Hornaday knew if the Zoo was to obtain the requisite new animals, he would need to rely, to some extent, on animal dealers. Nevertheless, Hornaday continued to send his curators out on expeditions as often as the Zoo could afford it. For at least a part of every

KING SNAKE

An expedition to Darwin Bay, Galápagos, 1925. Hornaday sent his curators out into the field as often as possible—in early years to collect specimens, and in later years to observe animals in the field.

year, Zoo curators traveled to such places as Nova Scotia, Florida, Mexico, and South America—wherever extraordinary animals could be found and safely shipped home. In general, Hornaday was distressed by the poor record of animal dealers, and he wanted his curators to do better. The least the Zoo could do, he felt, was to collect as much *information* as possible before they collected their animals.

Ditmars and Hornaday were delighted that the treasured liophis arrived in New York safe and healthy. In fact, of their large new collection of South American snakes, only one died

in transport. For 1906, that was phenomenal. Ditmars' years of carefully observing his snakes in the wild and at the Zoo and of recording impressions about their behavior and health were the key. These observations inspired him to design special boxes for the snakes' transport. Ditmars' boxes were better ventilated than the more primitive ones usually used for snake transport, and they allowed for the serpents to be given water each day. "Ventilation and water did the trick," Ditmars jotted in his notebook. It seems simple enough to us today, but at the time such careful observation and recording of information was an important step in improving the health and safety of captive animals.

Hornaday would no doubt be happy to learn that in the twenty-first century, the vast majority of animals added to zoo collections are zoo-born and bred. But at the turn of the *twentieth* century, while most zoos were still busy pillaging the wild in the interest of expanding their collections, a new idea had taken root and was beginning to blossom at the Bronx Zoo. Bronx Zoo scientists would begin observing animals in the wild—not with the goal of shipping them back to the Zoo but simply to gather information about those animals. Scientists would bring that information back to the Zoo and to a wider public so that the Zoo's animals might be better cared for from start to finish and people everywhere might begin to see the wild world in a new light.

THE CALL OF THE WILD

In 1916, Curator of Birds William Beebe and a few colleagues paddled up the Berbice River, through the hot, lush jungle of British Guiana (now called Guyana). In a tangle of thorn trees overlooking the river, he saw a few of the strange, rare birds he was hoping to find. They were hunkered down in the shade, trying to avoid the midafternoon heat. He noted their disheveled feathers, awkward flight, and croaking, froglike voices. In terms of their evolutionary development, these birds—called hoatzins—appear closer to their dinosaurian ancestry than any other living birds.

Beebe observed the whole area for some time, taking notes about the other plants and animals—insects, birds, and fish— that together made up the hoatzins' environment.

The hoatzin nests, he noted, were always built over water. Beebe approached one slowly. It was little more than a ramshackle platform of sticks, balanced between some thorn-tree limbs and hidden among the green foliage and wisteria-like blossoms. As Beebe's boat drew nearer, the mother remained on the nest, unconcerned. Through the sweet scent of the flowers Beebe began to smell the hoatzins' strong, musky odor. Finally, the mother hoatzin stood up, faced the boat, raised her wings and tail threateningly, and protested in her froglike voice. Pretty soon all the hoatzins within earshot were lifting their wings and tails and croaking in sympathy.

Curator of Birds William Beebe, on expedition in British Guiana in 1916.

The mother hoatzin held her ground as Beebe and his assistants took a few photographs. But when they tried moving even closer to the nest, she reluctantly flew off. The scrawny week-old nestling stood up and peered over the sticks of his nest. His mother—and father, too—looked on and croaked to him from a tangle of mangroves nearby.

The chick's flight feathers had not yet grown in completely, and his skimpy covering of dark feather-fuzz ruled out the possibility of flying off to join them. He craned his skinny neck up and surveyed the situation with big, intelligent eyes.

One of Beebe's assistants began climbing the thorn tree toward the nest, hoping to secure a specimen for further study. The branches shook. The little hoatzin stretched his wings up. Unlike any other living bird—but startlingly like the ancient and long-extinct *Archaeopteryx*—young hoatzins have hands on the front edges of their wings, equipped with strong, clawed fingers. The chick, Beebe observed, looked much like a young dinosaur or a miniature Galápagos tortoise.

The odd, reptilian-looking baby reached up and grasped a branch. Using both his hands and feet, he climbed farther up the tree, away from the curious scientist. The scientist pressed closer and grabbed the thorny branch just six feet away from where the chick had stopped. Sensing the danger, the chick put his last, and most surprising, defense into play. No

A hoatzin chick. These rare birds were the focus of Beebe's 1916 expedition to British Guiana.

spotted the familiar little head and scrawny neck stretching up out of the water near a bit of driftwood. Beebe paddled the boat toward the chick, but only halfheartedly, because by this time he had decided that this brave little evolutionary throwback deserved his freedom. The chick dove under again, only to reappear farther away from the boat under a tangle of vines. Five or six minutes later, the little bird reached one of its dinosaurian hands out of the water, grabbed on to a branch, and began the long climb! In fifteen minutes, it had hauled itself up the thorn tree and navigated, with unerring accuracy, back to its nest, while the mother hoatzin stood by, croaking her encouragement.

Hornaday hoped, eventually, to house some hoatzins at the Zoo, but Beebe was not going to ship this bird home. In fact, *he* had no plans of going home to New York anytime soon, either. Instead, he remained in Guyana, studying the hoatzins' environment. He had produced a paper entitled "Ecology of the Hoatzin" for the NYZS's scientific journal, *Zoologica,* and he would soon write a chapter on the subject for one of his most popular books, *Jungle Peace.* All across America, for the first time in history, tens of thousands of eager readers would be introduced to this amazing bird and to the wonders of its unique and fragile environment.

Hornaday was not entirely pleased at first. As far as he could tell, Beebe seemed more interested in staying away from the

other baby bird alive can accomplish such a feat—he stood up, stretched his wings straight back, leaned forward, and dove into the river.

Beebe and his crew watched in awe at the chick's miraculous escape. But how could the little creature have survived a fifteen-foot plummet to the muddy water below? They waited as the ripples disappeared where the chick had entered the water. Gradually the water became still, and still there was no sign of the chick.

Many minutes passed before Beebe finally

Zoo than in tending the animals he brought home. This made the usually grumpy, hard-driving director even grumpier. Hornaday had hoped his bird curator would stay home and take care of all the fascinating new birds he had collected, in the fabu-

> **"Before we can have the complete solution to the whys and wherefores of [certain kinds of animal behavior], there must be a great deal of uncomfortable climbing and diving, hiding in unpleasant places, getting wet and hot and cramped and weary."**

ZOOLOGICA

SCIENTIFIC CONTRIBUTIONS OF THE
NEW YORK ZOOLOGICAL SOCIETY

VOLUME I, NUMBERS 2, 3

ECOLOGY OF THE HOATZIN

AN ORNITHOLOGICAL RECONNAISSANCE
OF NORTHEASTERN VENEZUELA

By C. WILLIAM BEEBE
Curator of Birds

PUBLISHED BY THE SOCIETY
THE ZOOLOGICAL PARK, NEW YORK
DECEMBER 28, 1909

Beebe's article on the hoatzin ran in the Zoo's scientific journal.

lous new Bird House he had designed. But that was not to be. The practical aspects of zookeeping did not really interest Beebe, nor was he content to watch wild animals in captivity. Beebe's goal was to understand wildlife in the wild.

Hornaday knew that, apart from collecting new animals for the Zoo, the NYZS had excellent reasons to pursue scientific research in the field. And Beebe's writings were even more brilliant than his work as a curator. Hornaday had to admit it—in spite of the inconvenience to the Zoological Park of losing a good curator, Beebe was the best candidate for pursuing that research.

From early childhood, William Beebe had been interested in observing and describing wildlife. When he was eight years old, his family moved from Brooklyn, New York, to the then-rural town of East Orange, New Jersey. Many evenings he sat on the roof outside his upper-story bedroom window and listened to the calls of the different birds passing overhead. He watched them whenever he could, and he wrote many descriptions of them in his journal. When he was not out on his roof or hiking through the woods observing wildlife, he was reading books of exploration and wild adventure.

As a grown-up, Beebe believed in participating in the lives of the animals he studied as closely as the limitations of his lanky six-foot frame allowed. "Before we can have the complete solution to the whys and wherefores of [certain kinds of animal behavior], there must be a great deal of uncomfortable climbing and diving, hiding in unpleasant places, getting wet and hot and cramped and weary," he said in his book *Nonsuch: Land of Water.* "And then after we have tried to be sandpipers and ants, silver-sides and mackerel, we may attain to the honor of such knowledge as our prejudiced, but humbled minds will permit." In his famous essay "On Walden Pond," the early American philosopher Henry David Thoreau described becoming a "neighbor to the birds," not by putting them in cages but by building his own "cage" near them. Following in Thoreau's tradition, Beebe became the first research scientist to map out a single area and study its various species over a period of many years.

In 1916, Beebe established the first of his several research stations—a house on a wooded hill

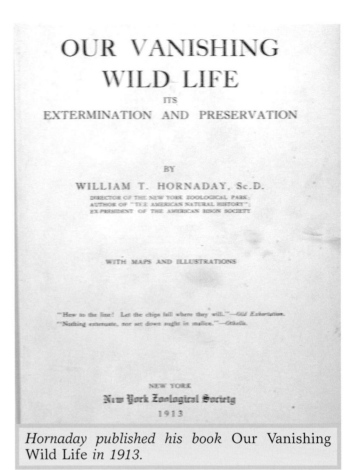

OUR VANISHING WILD LIFE
ITS
EXTERMINATION AND PRESERVATION

BY

WILLIAM T. HORNADAY, Sc.D.

DIRECTOR OF THE NEW YORK ZOOLOGICAL PARK;
AUTHOR OF "THE AMERICAN NATURAL HISTORY";
EX-PRESIDENT OF THE AMERICAN BISON SOCIETY

WITH MAPS AND ILLUSTRATIONS

"Hew to the line! Let the chips fall where they will."—*Old Exhortation.*
"Nothing extenuate, nor set down aught in malice."—*Othello.*

NEW YORK
New York Zoological Society
1913

Hornaday published his book Our Vanishing Wild Life *in 1913.*

overlooking the Mazaruni River, not too far from the Berbice, where he would continue to study the hoatzins and their environment. By 1922, the NYZS had named him their director of the Department of Tropical Research. From 1916 on (with a short leave to train American pilots in World War I), he was allowed to come and go at the Zoological Park as he pleased, and he had no pressing responsibilities to attend to there. He was free to wander and pursue his scientific research to his heart's content. The Zoo's adventuresome curator of birds was beginning his celebrated career as one of the greatest field scientists of the twentieth century.

The children of the 1910s, '20s, and '30s waited eagerly to hear the radio reports or to read the exciting magazine articles and books about William Beebe's adventures. In 1913, William Hornaday published his book *Our Vanishing Wild Life*. It was one of the very first books to pursue the subject of endangered wildlife, and it became quite popular. Beebe wrote a special chapter for that book entitled "Destruction of Birds in the Far East," which describes his seventeen-month expedition in 1909–10 to study and collect the pheasants of Asia and the East Indies. In it he predicts the ultimate extinction

Raymond Ditmars, curator of reptiles, with an iguana. While Beebe was interested mainly in field research, Ditmars focused on the animals in his care at the Zoo.

By 1949, William Beebe (left) set up his last tropical field station, Simla, located in the Arima Valley of Trinidad.

of many species if wasteful hunting practices go uncurtailed. Through his many writings, Beebe gave most people their first vivid understanding not only of jungles but of a wide variety of unfamiliar habitats—from the high Himalayas to the depths of the sea. And he gave them their first indication that the unique animals in those habitats might one day be gone.

While Beebe was turning his attention to the field, Ditmars began to turn most of his efforts to the observation of the animals in his charge. He wanted others to have the close-up look at animal behavior that he was able to have as a curator. In 1916, as Beebe was setting up his first tropical field station, Ditmars began pursuing an entirely new way of getting people interested in zoology.

Today we can switch on the television and find any number of dazzling films about wild animals in their world. We can watch pandas foraging in the bamboo forests of China, condors sailing over the high Andes, chimpanzees at home in the jungles of Africa—wherever wild animals dwell, film crews have trekked in to film them.

But in 1916? Country children may have hunted squirrels and rabbits in their backyards, like William Hornaday did as a youngster out on the Iowa prairie. But creatures like the fish-eating liophis lived in a world apart—far beyond the imagination of any American child. In the early twentieth century, there was no television, and even movies were still considered rather newfangled. (The first widely seen silent film in America did not come out until 1915.) At first, William Hornaday was skeptical about whether animal movies would be of much use to anyone. But Ditmars had his own ideas. He began by taking moving pictures of his favorite creatures—reptiles—moving about at night and of baby snakes hatching out of their eggs, natural events he knew people rarely had a chance to observe. Soon he went on to take moving pictures of the larger animals at the Zoo. The NYZS board members, and even the skeptical Hornaday himself, were delighted by his efforts.

Several short nature films, created with the goal of educating viewers about the lives and habits of animals, had been made during the late 1890s and early 1900s, but they were mostly dull, static productions that never achieved much popularity. With his unique sense of fun and drama, Ditmars managed to make his films both educational and entertaining. Over the course of several years, he produced a collection of forty-three films, called the Living Natural History series. Thousands of children flocked to the Zoological Park with their teachers and parents to enjoy Ditmars' new educational wildlife movies. Before long, his films were being shown in schools and theaters all across the country.

Both Beebe's writings and Ditmars' films fired up popular interest, which in turn greatly helped the cause Hornaday lived for: the preservation of wild animals. While some zoo critics today say the availability of good books and nature programs on TV makes zoos obsolete, it's important to remember that it was zoo curators who produced the first exciting books and nature films that helped make the plight of wild animals a popular cause.

In 1916, a new age of awareness was dawning, and at its forefront were pioneering Bronx Zoo scientists William Beebe and Raymond Ditmars. A few early naturalists and conservationists were the first to awaken to the shocking realization of how threatened wild animals were—all over the world—as a result of human activities. Now, through the efforts of Beebe and Ditmars and others like them, the Bronx Zoo was helping make sure that awareness would spread to all.

THE NEW ZOO

In 1926, at the age of seventy-two, William Hornaday retired as director of the New York Zoological Park. The NYZS's Board of Directors was probably right when it declared that the Bronx Zoo, under Hornaday's direction, had become "the largest and most beautiful, the most popular and the most widely known zoological park in the world."

But when the Zoo's renowned veterinarian, Dr. W. Reid Blair, stepped in to fill Hornaday's position, controversy began. One of Dr. Blair's first suggestions was that they might try creating a new barless exhibit. Some of the newer zoos around the world were designing exhibits that used deep moats, rather than bars, to keep the animals contained. While visiting these exhibits, zoo-goers had an unimpeded view of wild animals interacting with one another in a spacious, natural setting. Needless to say, the zoos that had added such new exhibits were becoming more and more popular.

Ironically, in spite of his early goal of presenting animals in their natural surroundings, the still-fiery Hornaday sent a protest letter from his retirement desk in Connecticut. Such silly, faddish ideas, he claimed, were not for the New York Zoological Park! In such exhibits, he said, the animals are too far away from the visitors, making close study of them impossible. Blair snapped back, "If we do not use up all our energy in trying to maintain that we have spoken the last word in zoological building and exhibition, we may be able to pick up a few ideas worth considering from time to time." Unfortunately, most of the old, founding members of the NYZS agreed with Hornaday. After all, the most popular zoo in the world had been created under their guidance and administration. Why would anyone want to change it now? By 1929, the Great Depression had begun, and economic hard times made it even harder for

most famous founders, Henry Fairfield Osborn—decided the time had come "to break up the old patterns."

As a young boy growing up in New Jersey in the 1890s, Fairfield Osborn created his first zoo—in his bedroom. He kept a variety of bugs, white mice, a flying squirrel, ring-necked doves, and even a baby alligator, who used to crawl into bed with him every night. The baby especially liked to settle himself down on Fair's tummy, chirping "Ungh, ungh, ungh," just as he would have chirped for his mother in the wild, until he'd gotten all snug and comfortable.

Later, when he was president of one of the most famous zoos in the world, Osborn's empathy for animals became legendary. He frequently strolled through the Zoo, often getting stalled near the Lion House or the Sea Lion Pool or some other exhibit. If there were children around, he couldn't resist telling them about the animals. One day, as he was passing the polar bears, he stopped, pointed to one,

Fairfield Osborn was elected president of the New York Zoological Society in 1941.

the younger members to pursue new ideas.

In 1940, Dr. Blair retired, and Fairfield Osborn was soon elected president of the NYZS. By then, the economy had finally begun to revive, and Osborn—son of one of the Zoo's

"Our gorillas don't receive enough affection. They're intelligent and sensitive and lonesome. We must see that the keepers embrace them more, treat them like human babies."

and remarked to the keeper, "That bear's unhappy." The keeper said he hadn't noticed anything wrong with him. "Nevertheless," said Osborn, "he is unhappy." He asked one of the Zoo veterinarians to give the bear a checkup. Just as Osborn had suspected, the bear was not well. He had developed a serious skin infection.

By temperament, Osborn was naturally sensitive to animals and their needs. But his deeper understanding of animal behavior came from the kind of close observation that cura-

A gorilla named Oka with keeper Mickey Quinn. The Zoo's gorillas began to thrive once they received more affection from their keepers.

tors like Raymond Ditmars had pioneered. Gorillas have always been among the most difficult animals to keep. Director Hornaday had had strict ideas of what foods would be good for them, but for the most part they refused to cooperate. Two or three died within a year after arriving. Hornaday quickly responded, giving up the idea of collecting more gorillas. Osborn studied the problem. "I think I know what's wrong," he concluded. "Our gorillas don't receive enough affection. They're intelligent and sensitive and lonesome. We must see that the keepers embrace them more, treat them like human babies." With plenty of hugs from their keepers, the Zoo's gorillas finally began to eat and thrive.

After making the animals happy, Osborn's most treasured goal was to help zoo-goers learn about the animals' natural habitats. From the beginning, he took what he termed a "zoo-geographic" approach to zoo design. Before Osborn's time, the old pattern was to group animals according to type: There was the Monkey House, the Reptile House, the Small Mammal House, the Lion House, and others. Although a few zoos were making changes, this style of organization was still solidly in place at most zoos around the world. Instead, Osborn insisted, wherever possible, on showing animals grouped according to their geographical origins: for example, dry African savannas, tropical South American jungles, or high Himalayan mountains.

Whereas Hornaday and his contemporaries ultimately decided that zoo-goers needed to see animals up close, Osborn felt there was far greater educational value in showing animals behaving naturally in their natural environments. And he knew it would be better for the animals, too. William Beebe's field research had deepened the Zoo's understanding of how habitats, or ecosystems, work. All of the plants and animals that make up any ecosystem are dependent upon one another. From the largest predators to the simplest plants eaten by the smallest plant-eaters—all parts of an ecosystem must be healthy for that ecosystem to survive. This was a critical new insight, and Osborn wanted that understanding

"The African Plains," created by Fairfield Osborn, opened on May 1, 1941, and is still one of the Zoo's most popular exhibits.

The Zoo's own pride of lions.

to be conveyed by the Zoo's new exhibits.

One of the first things he did as president was to create a barless exhibit—the first of the really modern exhibits at the Zoo. "The African Plains" opened on May 1, 1941. Today the African Plains is still one of the most popular exhibits. Just a short stroll from the Zoo's southern entrance, visitors can look out over

Nyalas grazing in "The African Plains" under the watchful eye of a lion. Predators are actually separated from the prey animals by hidden moats.

an African savanna—an open grassland, or prairie, environment. As in Africa, the Zoo's savanna has its pride of lions. They groom one another, mate, raise their cubs, and watch the herds of zebras, nyalas, blesbok, and Thomson's gazelles that naturally occupy the savanna with them. But you won't see them hunting. Even though they appear to be living side by side on the prairie, the prey animals are separated from the predators by carefully concealed moats. In 1941, Osborn's African Plains was among the most realistic-looking moated exhibits ever created. He even had his designers trim and crop the native shrubs and bushes to resemble acacia trees and other savanna plants. Many of the animal groupings from Hornaday's time—monkeys, reptiles, rodents, and more—still exist at the Zoo today. But after the African Plains, all the exhibits began to reflect Osborn's determination to get the public interested in wild ecosystems.

Unfortunately, by 1941 people had more to think about than exciting new zoo exhibits:

World War II was in full swing. All around the globe, geographical areas that escaped bombing and trampling by tanks and troops were being plundered for their fuel and natural resources. The desperate state of the world made Fairfield Osborn feel even more keenly the urgent necessity of teaching people about ecosystems and how they work. He was among the first to alert the general public to the ways in which ecosystems were being threatened. In his seminal book, *Our Plundered Planet*, he explained how over-population, depletion of natural resources such as soil and forests, and the wide-reaching effects of World War II were causing tremendous, possibly irreversible damage to wild animals and their habitats.

Osborn dedicated the rest of his life to alerting the world to this crisis. He expanded upon Hornaday's ideas of wildlife conservation: While continuing Hornaday's work to stop wasteful hunting practices, he worked against the wasteful use and abuse of soil, forests, air, and water as well.

The Jackson Hole Wildlife Park in Wyoming, established in 1946.

Grand Teton National Park gave scientists a place to do long-term wildlife research.

Much like Hornaday, Osborn was not content to merely build educational exhibits at the Zoo. In 1948, he helped charter the Conservation Foundation as a part of the Zoo's conservation department. (This eventually led to today's World Wildlife Fund, the world's largest privately financed conservation organization.) The Foundation published books and articles and produced films that helped people in the United States understand the ways in which their activities were threatening wild animals and the environment. Nothing like the Conservation Foundation had ever existed before. Today we owe much of our awareness of environmental problems to the Foundation's pioneering efforts.

Beyond books and films and zoo exhibits, Osborn believed people needed a wild *place* where they could actually experience a vital and robust ecosystem. By 1924, moose, mule deer, pronghorn antelopes, and white-tailed deer could be found at the Bronx Zoo, but their herds had nearly vanished from the green valleys and snowy peaks of the Grand Tetons, where they had once flourished. In 1946, Fairfield Osborn and Laurance Rockefeller, then a vice president of the

49

A grizzly bear in Yellowstone National Park.

NYZS, helped create the Jackson Hole Wildlife Park in Wyoming. It was a completely new type of park. About 400 of the park's acres were fenced so visitors could watch the wildlife. Coyotes, American bison, black bears, and even grizzly bears could often be spotted in this protected area. As the populations of wildlife increased, ordinary visitors could come to soak in the natural beauty and marvel at the animals. An additional 33,000 acres of wilderness nearby, presented by John D. Rockefeller, Jr., became the nucleus of Grand Teton National Park. Here field scientists finally had a place to pursue long-term biological research. Wildlife research still goes on in this unique and spectacularly beautiful area, some of it still supported by the Zoo.

For the next few decades, Fairfield Osborn, William Beebe, and other NYZS scientists would be busy getting the word out: If we exterminate even one species of plant or animal in an ecosystem, if we deplete the soil, or if we pollute the air or water, we threaten to destroy that ecosystem completely. But along with spreading the word, Osborn and the NYZS decided that one of their main goals for the second half of the twentieth century would be to figure out how to help restore some of those damaged ecosystems—not only in the United States but in countries all around the world.

> Zoos have no validity nowadays, no purpose, except to help protect and raise endangered animals and to raise public consciousness about the plight of wildlife.
>
> —George B. Schaller

REACHING OUT TO THE WORLD

Fairfield Osborn observed that the gorillas under his care needed lots of hugs. But in the mid-twentieth century, no one knew much about how these animals lived in the wild. The mountain gorillas of central Africa were a particular mystery. Osborn and others at the New York Zoological Society knew that the human population in this area was exploding, and wild lands were quickly being converted to farmlands. Osborn feared that these rare and fascinating animals were endangered.

Exactly how many of them were left? What did they eat? How did they interact with each other? What kinds of damage had their ecosystem sustained as a result of human activities? George B. Schaller, then a graduate student at the University of Wisconsin, helped organize an expedition to Africa to try to answer these questions. Osborn and the NYZS agreed to sponsor the expedition. Along with support from the National Science Foundation and the Institute of the Parks of the Congo, the world's first long-term, in-depth study of mountain gorillas began.

In February 1959, Schaller and his wife, Kay Schaller, arrived in Rumangabo, the headquarters for what was then called Albert National Park. Established by the government of the Belgian Congo in 1925, the park encompassed the rugged terrain of the Virunga Volcanoes, along the border between Rwanda and eastern Congo (now part of the Democratic

George B. Schaller. The NYZS financed Schaller's expedition to Africa for the purpose of studying gorillas—it was the world's first in-depth study of gorillas.

Republic of the Congo). (Today Albert Park has been divided into Virunga National Park in the Democratic Republic of the Congo and Volcanoes National Park in Rwanda.) Once they'd gotten settled in the small guesthouse in the park, Schaller hiked through the cold, drizzly high-altitude jungle around the volcanoes and searched for gorillas. Over the course of several days, he had plenty of time to recall the stories explorers had told of the gorillas' fierce, aggressive behavior. Finally one morning he

A gorilla in the Congo.

> **"Constant vigilance must be maintained to prevent a disastrous tip of the balance from security to extinction."**

heard a wild, half-screaming roar, which he said shattered the stillness of the forest and made the hairs of his neck stand on end. He was on the trail of his first gorilla group. Although Schaller said he never got used to the sudden, breathtaking sound of a male gorilla's roar, he discovered that they are not the dark, frightening creatures many had imagined. The gorillas soon came to tolerate his presence as he observed them day after day. He learned that they live in close-knit social groups and are much more peaceful and gentle than people had previously thought. Osborn had certainly been correct in his understanding that the Zoo's gorillas needed plenty of social contact. But Schaller's study was the first to describe the kinds of social groups gorillas formed in nature.

He watched as the gorilla families foraged for wild celery, stinging nettles, and bamboo shoots. Back in the 1920s, Hornaday had called one of his gorillas an "unmitigated numskull" when she refused the luscious bananas he offered and instead seemed more interested in devouring the stems and the inner linings of the peels. No doubt Hornaday would have been interested to see the diet mountain gorillas enjoy in the wild! Perhaps Rwandan banana farmers felt even more frustrated than Hornaday when—as often happened—gorilla groups raided their orchards, eating the stems and peels and tossing the fruit aside. Schaller estimated that there were between 400 and 500 mountain gorillas left in the park. He noted that much of the land where gorillas once roamed and foraged had been cleared and plowed by local farmers. Sadly, even some of the land that had previously been set aside as parkland was gone, and villagers often felt they had no choice but to kill gorillas that raided their crops. To make matters worse, illegal grazing of cattle in the park was stripping the vegetation in many areas, and illegal hunting was reducing the gorillas' already declining numbers.

By 1963, Schaller finished writing the world's first detailed study of mountain gorillas. The Zoo's curators finally had a true picture of the kind of family groups they would have to nurture if they wanted their gorillas to thrive and breed in captivity. But how much natural habitat would they need to continue to live healthy lives in the wild? And how could what was left of their ecosystem be preserved?

Like Beebe, Schaller soon became a widely

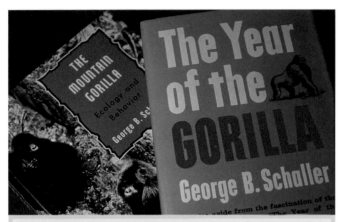

Schaller's popular book The Year of the Gorilla *gave millions a window into gorilla behavior and life in the jungle as it drew upon the insights of his more scholarly book* The Mountain Gorilla.

admired nature writer. In his popular book *The Year of the Gorilla,* millions of readers had a chance to explore the African jungle with him and experience gorilla life. Many came to understand the political and economic pressures that threatened the gorillas and their habitat.

While Beebe had been a close observer and a brilliant reporter, bringing home the news about wild ecosystems around the world, Schaller and his sponsors at the NYZS wanted to go further. They felt the time had come to step in with practical advice, education, and aid for countries like Congo and Rwanda to help them preserve their wild lands.

Over the next few decades, the human population would continue to grow. Useful farmland and rich hunting and grazing areas would

be even more in demand. How could naturalists from a faraway country ask that some of the Rwandans' most fertile land be set aside for the welfare of animals when Rwandan children were going hungry? The only way to save the gorillas was to work with the local people, to help meet their needs first. With a united effort, perhaps humans could continue to preserve the gorillas and save their threatened ecosystem. In 1963, Schaller declared, "Constant vigilance must be maintained to prevent a disastrous tip of the balance from security to extinction." And this is still true today, for the animals in Rwanda as well as in other countries.

Not long after Schaller finished writing his books about the mountain gorillas, the director of the Serengeti National Park in Tanzania asked him to come observe lions. As with the mountain gorillas, no one had yet attempted a serious long-term study of lions. Naturalists knew that lions, too, were endangered. But how many were left? What were their daily lives like? And what would it take to ensure their survival? These were some of the questions the park's director and the people of Tanzania hoped Schaller could help them answer.

Even more than gorillas and humans, lions and humans have had a hard time living side by side in peace. By the 1920s, lions in northern Africa had completely vanished. Like the bison in North America, they were hunted out of existence by their human neighbors. But while Hornaday and many of the big-game hunters of his time had been eager to help the buffalo, antelopes, deer, and other large herbivores, the idea of preserving wolves, mountain lions, and other predatory animals was not widely accepted. Besides being considered dangerous to humans and their farm animals, they were often seen as competing with humans for wild game. Lions survived south of the Sahara

A lioness eats her kill, a zebra. In Hornaday's time, preserving predatory animals was not as widely embraced as preserving big herbivores, such as buffalo and zebras.

Desert, partly because it was remote and not many European, American, or other foreign hunting parties had managed to get there yet.

In 1929, the Tanzanian government designated 900 square miles around the village of Seronera as a game reserve and, fortunately, by 1937 the hunting of lions was outlawed there. In 1941—the same year Fairfield Osborn imported a little spot of the Serengeti to New York City in the form of the Zoo's African Plains exhibit—this reserve became the core of the amazing 5,700-square-mile Serengeti National Park.

At about the same time that Schaller began his field studies in Africa, Osborn promoted his energetic curator of birds, William G. Conway, to be director of the Zoo. Soon Conway took on the duties of general director of the NYZS as well, and the Society's worldwide conservation efforts continued to grow.

In 1965, under Conway's leadership, the NYZS, together with Rockefeller University, created the Institute for Research in Animal Behavior. With the support of the Institute, the NYZS appointed three field scientists to pursue research in different ecosystems. Already admired for his work with the mountain gorillas and just getting started with his work in the Serengeti, George Schaller was their first appointee.

On many occasions Schaller experienced first-hand the importance of the protection the Serengeti National Park provided for lions and its other wildlife. For three years, he and his

William G. Conway became general director of the NYZS in 1966.

wife and their two young sons, Mark and Eric, lived in a yellow house with a tin roof near park headquarters in Seronera. Giraffes often came to browse at the acacia tree in their front yard, and gazelles sometimes raided their garden. Every day Schaller drove or hiked from his home to the wide, golden savanna to observe lions roaming, hunting, socializing, mating, and raising their cubs. Every day he recorded his observations carefully in his notebooks.

At the beginning of his study, in the autumn of 1966, Schaller marked 156 lions with ear tags

Lions and cubs, Africa.

so he could plot their movements in the field. He did not like tagging any more than was absolutely necessary, but one November day two years later he found himself holding one of those silver ear tags in his hands. It was covered in lion's blood. Without the tag, he might never have known what happened to one of his favorite lions. This lion had roamed outside the park's boundary and was shot by members of a hunting party. The outfitter of the hunt returned the tag to Schaller at the park's head-quarters, believing he had done nothing wrong. Some hunting was allowed outside the park's borders, and many people still felt that killing a big predator was a triumph over nature.

In many parts of the world, even in national parks, lions and other big cats were still being shot, with the idea that this would actually benefit the other wildlife. Schaller believed that predators had a positive effect on wildlife, and he helped show the world that when predators are eliminated from an ecosystem, that ecosystem

Each lion is an individual.

is thrown out of balance. Plant-eaters soon over-populate and devastate the plant life. Then mature plant-eaters become weak and sickly, and youngsters die slowly of starvation. "The lion and other predators are an integral part of the ecological community," he observed, "and must be present if the prey animals are to survive in all their vigor and abundance."

During his years in the Serengeti, Schaller had gotten to know many of the lions as individuals. He worried about their problems and thought about what the future might bring them. The human population would continue to grow, putting the lands bordering the park into ever greater demand for agriculture. The park's rangers would need to keep after the countless poachers who snared lions, sometimes merely

for their skins and claws, which were sold as rugs and trinkets.

The young male lion's death at the hands of a trophy hunter—a proud, beautiful animal killed not for food or self-protection, since the park's lions had become relatively tame around humans, but so that his lifeless hide could hang on someone's wall—saddened Schaller more than he could express. Getting to know the Serengeti's lions made it all the more clear to him how vital the park was, not only as a place for lions but as a place where humans could stop to observe these magnificent creatures, to suppress for a moment the unthinking urge to kill and renew their sense of wonder and feeling of oneness with the wild. When his books on the Serengeti lions came out, they were the first to describe the wild lives of lions. The stories of his adventures held readers spellbound and, like the stories of the mountain gorillas, made them aware of the social and economic pressures working against the lions in the great Serengeti Park.

Dr. Schaller's approach to studying wildlife—his empathy toward the animals and his meticulous attention to details over a long period of time—became the model for the NYZS's field researchers. In 1972, William Conway appointed Schaller to be the NYZS's coordinator of field science on five continents.

Across the span of five decades, Dr. Schaller has helped protect more wildlife and more wild places than any other human alive today. And he has made it clear to the many conservation biologists who have followed in his footsteps that although it is one thing to study a particular ecosystem and learn what must be done to preserve it, they must also include the needs of the people who live in and around that environment and provide them with conservation education as well as help with the ongoing management of their wild lands and the surrounding areas. Some NYZS scientists have advised how to open parks to ecotourism or how to harvest resources from wild lands without depleting their resources or harming the land, so that countries can gain economic sustenance from their national wildlife treasures while giving the animals the wilderness they need to survive.

With help and funding from the NYZS, conservation biologists have sought to maintain the constant vigilance Schaller foresaw would be necessary. Alan Rabinowitz has expanded Schaller's fight to preserve habitats for big cats, focusing especially on the jaguars of South America. Bill Weber and Amy Vedder have worked closely with the government and people in Rwanda for many years to ensure the preservation of the mountain gorillas. In spite of wars, internal conflicts, economic pressures, and fear of famine that continue to force the people to turn some of their wild lands into farmlands, gorillas and big cats have managed to hang on with the help of their human neighbors. Today more than sixty scientists and a hundred researchers with the NYZS (renamed the Wildlife Conservation Society, or WCS, in 1993) assist local scientists in over fifty countries worldwide.

But throughout the 1960s, while the NYZS was busy establishing a truly international presence, making sure that wild ecosystems stayed intact, the Zoo itself lagged behind. It remained self-centered, proudly proclaiming itself the biggest and best zoo in the world, while offering little by way of assistance to other, less successful zoos. Hornaday had once declared the American Association of Zoological Parks and Aquariums—the main organization through which American zoos assist each other and exchange ideas—a bunch of "inexperienced upstarts." And the Bronx Zoo still had the reputation of being cool and aloof to others. The gregarious new director, William Conway, was determined to see that change.

THE FUTURE OF THE ZOO

The water of the Laguna Colorado in Bolivia is blood-red, and the volcanic mountains that surround this shimmering, shallow lake are dusted year-round in snow. High in the Andes Mountains, this is one of the harshest environments on Earth. Here you can find a rare and beautiful species of bird—James'

Today the Zoo is home to many flamingos, including Chilean flamingos, which are close relatives of the James'.

61

flamingos. They are drawn to the Laguna Colorado because the algae that stain its water red are one of their favorite foods.

If you can reach this remote area during the breeding season in December, you might have an opportunity to view flocks of James' flamingos preparing for their annual nesting. In 1960, scientists knew little about these birds. But in December of that year, William Conway, along with a photographer and a Chilean scientist as their guide, camped on the shores of the lake in hopes of learning more. After days of struggling with unwieldy nets in the whipping cold winds, Conway finally devised a way to capture a few flamingos by anchoring simple loops of fishing line underwater where the flamingos

Conway (right) devised a way to capture a few James' flamingos using fishing line, Laguna Colorado, Bolivia, 1960.

Conway (right) building flamingo nests at the Zoo, 1958.

liked to wade. The Bronx Zoo became the first zoo in the world where people could see and learn about this remarkable bird.

In keeping with the Zoo's time-honored tradition, however, it was not enough to celebrate a new exhibition of birds at the Zoo while forgetting about those in the wild. Human activities, such as mining and hunting, were beginning to endanger the James' flamingos' fragile ecosystem. In 1961, with the guidance of the NYZS, Conway helped set up the Laguna Colorado Reserve so that at least one of the flamingos' favorite breeding grounds would be protected. Human activities still threaten this area. But since Conway's first expedition, NYZS/WCS scientists have continued to study the flamingos and to work for their conservation in this and other parts of South America.

Chilean flamingos enjoying their pond at the Bronx Zoo.

If you can't make it to Bolivia, you can still see flamingos from South America wading in the pond at the Dancing Crane Café at the Zoo. You might see them reach their long necks down, dipping the tops of their heads into the water to filter out the nutritious algae with the comblike bristles in their bills. And you might even see William Conway standing beside you. Ever since his early days as the Zoo's curator of birds,

flamingos have been one of his favorite animals. Choosing a favorite must have been difficult, though, since animals have been the passion of his life for as long as he can remember.

When he was only four years old, he began catching butterflies around his suburban neighborhood, outside St. Louis, Missouri. By the time he had finished elementary school, his butterfly collection had grown to a respectable size, and he gave it to his school as a graduation present. In junior high, he learned how to navigate three streetcar routes from his home to the St. Louis Zoo. He spent as much time there as he could. Eventually the zoo staff simply put him on the payroll, giving him a part-time job as a keeper's assistant. He went on to study biology at Washington University in St. Louis, but the zoo appointed him their bird curator even before his graduation. In 1956, the Bronx Zoo recruited him to be their assistant bird curator, and Conway welcomed the opportunity.

Whereas Schaller's aim was, like Beebe's, to study wildlife in the wild, William Conway, much like Raymond Ditmars, felt drawn to the Zoo. In 1966, he became president of the American Association of Zoological Parks and Aquariums (founded in 1924, and now called the American Zoo and Aquarium Association, or AZA). One can almost imagine the fiery-tempered Hornaday penning a letter of complaint from the grave at the very idea of the Bronx Zoo's director hobnobbing with such upstarts. But Conway saw that, in the long run, the Bronx Zoo could do more for the world's wildlife by helping other zoos than by competing over which zoo was best. By that time the NYZS's primary goal was the preservation of the world's fast-vanishing wild. Conway wanted to make sure that the Bronx Zoo, and all zoos, contributed to that goal as well—doing whatever they could within their own fences.

An Asian elephant calf with its mother.

Behind the scenes, zoo scientists today keep busy breeding new generations of zoo animals, including many endangered species. Zoo curators can no longer roam the world on collecting expeditions as Conway and others did in the past. The rarity of so many species in the wild and the fragility of their habitats make collecting no longer feasible, or even morally defensible.

A collecting party of the kind commonly led by animal dealers in the twentieth century could all but destroy what little remains of some animal populations today. Conscientious zoos will take an animal from the wild only in situations where the animal's life would be in jeopardy otherwise.

"Once there were vast numbers of dodo birds. 'Civilized' man killed them all—not one remains alive. Hence the expression 'Dead as a Dodo.' "

Over the last century, zoo scientists—veterinarians and keepers alike—have amassed a wealth of information about breeding and maintaining their animals in captivity. In the 1980s, Conway helped establish the AZA's Species Survival Plans (SSPs) for a number of endangered species. Under an SSP, an endangered species gets the benefit of all the knowledge of the many zoos that have worked with that type of animal. All members of the AZA share information, genetic material, and animals as they try to improve their breeding success and provide better care in every way. AZA's philosophy for the future is to encourage zoos to reduce the number of species they show and to concentrate their attention on keeping a few species well.

Today William Hornaday's hundred-year-old vision of captive breeding is finally successful. Nevertheless, SSPs do more to help zoos maintain the animals in their collections than they do to increase the number of animals in the wild. Most zoo-bred animals cannot be successfully introduced into their wild environments. They are too tame—too used to human ways. Breeding programs for the reintroduction of animals into the wild can be better established in rural areas with large tracts of land, such as the Bronx Zoo's breeding facility on St. Catherine's Island off the coast of Georgia. There the animals have plenty of space, and their lives are close to what they might be in the wild. Some animals can be born and raised in large facilities like St. Catherine's and then introduced successfully into their natural environment. In emergency situations, a good zoo breeding program may help rescue a few species from the brink of extinction.

Zoo critics will always question whether it is possible to *ever* justify exhibiting a wild animal. Just as Hornaday did, Conway took that question to heart. Regardless of how safe, healthy, and comfortable a zoo might keep an animal, that animal has been kept away from its natural home to be put on display for curious humans. Was a zoo's ability to maintain a breeding population justification enough for that zoo to continue to exist? Zoo breeding, no matter how successful at saving species, cannot save endangered habitats.

Conway asked himself if the Bronx Zoo's exhibits inspired in visitors a feeling of respect and wonder for the animals. Would people leave the Zoo with a deeper understanding of the animals and their ecosystems? Would they be motivated to help animals struggling to survive in endangered environments? If so, then Conway believed the Zoo could remain viable. But that was a big "if." A lot of work needed to be done before the Bronx Zoo could become an effective model for the future.

Conway began to put a stronger emphasis on the Zoo's longtime goal of educating its visitors about the wild. In the 1960s, the Bronx Zoo became the first zoo to direct visitors' attention to endangered species. The antelope skull later became a popular symbol for endangered species, and many zoos used it. But at that time the Bronx Zoo tagged each endangered animal's exhibit sign with a red "Dead as a Dodo" warning. Other signs positioned nearby explained the dodo symbol: "Once there were vast numbers of dodo birds. 'Civilized' man killed them all—not one remains alive. Hence the expression 'Dead as a Dodo.' Many other animals may be as dead as the dodo unless we protect them. This red symbol calls attention to endangered species. Look for it around the Bronx Zoo. And think about what it means—the final emptiness of extinction."

Like Osborn, Conway believed that if people could be shown, firsthand, the full beauty and complexity of an animal's environment, they would be inspired to protect it. Although an exotic *animal* may draw curious people to a zoo, a good zoo, he felt, must be dedicated to educating visitors about the benefits of preserving these animals' *habitats*. When Osborn

LESSER BIRD OF PARADISE

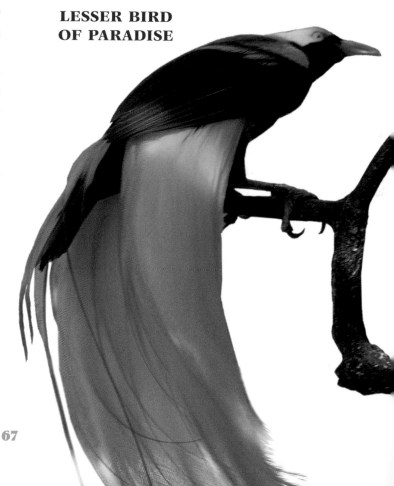

opened the African Plains exhibit in 1941, he took the first giant step toward creating more naturalistic, habitat-based exhibits at the Zoo. During the last half of the twentieth century, Conway and his staff designed and built some of the most innovative natural habitat exhibits in the world.

In the World of Birds, no barriers come between visitors and the wildlife. This is an indoor exhibit, so rather than moats, special lighting and the enticements of their simulated habitats keep the birds from flying into the visitors' areas. The habitats range from native New York woodland to South American rain

Gibbon on vine. The JungleWorld exhibit was the Zoo's first immersion exhibit.

QUETZAL

forest. As visitors stand before a lush re-creation of a New Guinea jungle, they might see the male bird of paradise fluffing up his brilliantly colored tufts and plumes to impress the females. Visitors will learn about the bird's ecosystem, and they will learn that the bird of paradise is endangered. The NYZS worked hard getting laws passed in New Guinea to outlaw the hunting of this bird, whose feathers were once prized as fashion accessories.

Anyone with the patience to linger long enough to take in the beauty of each habitat may also discover bee-eaters, toucans, quetzals, sun bitterns, and many others. Each flick of a feather or rustle of a leaf reveals another. Some zip past quickly—a blur of color across one's field of view. Others stand motionless and nearly invisible against the background of native vegetation. Conway's beloved mentor, William Beebe, who designed the Zoo's first Bird House in 1905, would no doubt have been delighted with this creative new exhibit. The World of Birds was so successful that between its opening in 1972 and the end of the twentieth century, Conway and his staff created several more exhibits emphasizing ecosystems and the interconnectedness of life.

In the 1970s, the first "landscape immersion" exhibits opened at the Woodland Park Zoo in Seattle. In a landscape immersion exhibit, rather than standing before a stage setting of an ecosystem, visitors find themselves, to one extent or another, actually surrounded by the ecosystem. The Bronx Zoo's first immersion exhibit opened in 1985. In his design for JungleWorld, Conway hoped to bring visitors as close as they were ever likely to get to a real walk through Southeast Asian jungle habitats. As visitors stroll through the four different environments, they can hear native birds and insects calling. They can feel the warm, misty air, smell the sweet earth, and listen to the waterfall splashing. They might even get caught in a thunderstorm. Colorful butterflies drift here and there through a rich array of tropical plant life. Leopards, silvered langurs, white-cheeked gibbons, tapirs, fruit bats, and binturongs are only a few of JungleWorld's animal inhabitants. In this—the first exhibit in the world to house so many different species under one roof—the more carefully you look, the more you will see.

CARMINE BEE-EATER

Gibbons (hanging) and tapirs are among the many animals that inhabit the JungleWorld exhibit.

As visitors leave the exhibit, exhilarated by the beauty and variety of rain forest life, they soon spot the Jungle Countdown clocks. Over half of all the plant and animal species on Earth today live in rain forests. But rain forests take up only 6 percent of Earth's land area. As the countdown clocks show, tropical rain forests are being cut down by humans for lumber and for farmland at a rate of about 100 acres per minute. Nearby, the Human Population clock keeps a record of Earth's pop-ulation: over 6 billion and increasing at a rate of approximately 180 people per minute. The effect is overwhelming. Can rain forests and their inhabitants withstand the human onslaught? In creating JungleWorld, Conway was driven by the hope that the more people know, the more willing and able they will be to meet the tremendous challenge of preserving what little rain forest is left.

In the Zoo's Congo Gorilla Forest, opened in 1999, gorillas can finally be seen as Dr.

Schaller and his associates were able to see them—foraging for their food, playing, taking care of their babies, and even expressing curiosity about and "talking" with their human visitors.

Before people understood much about gorillas and their complex needs, zoos tried to keep them secure in what amounted to dismal, concrete-lined pens. Zookeepers were afraid the gorillas would rip up any trees or bushes they planted. They worried that the gorillas might eat the display plants and become sick. In those now-outmoded exhibits, gorillas were often viewed by visitors as aggressive, crazed, or listless creatures. In the Congo Gorilla Forest, Conway's vision of a true immersion experience has become a reality. Visitors walk through a glass tunnel, getting a close-up view of one of the largest breeding groups of lowland gorillas in any zoo. Their lives are as close as

An adult gorilla babysits three youngsters.

A visitor looks at a juvenile gorilla through the glass.

possible to what they would be in their jungle environment. Visitors have the opportunity to get a genuine sense of what gorillas are, how they live, and the amazing variety of other creatures that share their endangered ecosystem. As they leave the Congo Gorilla Forest, visitors learn about some of the environmental problems in central Africa as well.

Critics have pointed out that it is not terribly helpful for zoos to draw people's attention to conservation issues and to evoke their concern, while leaving them without any means of doing something useful with that concern. A good zoo, Conway insists, offers visitors creative ways to channel the interest the zoo has aroused in them. In the Congo Gorilla Forest, zoo-goers are asked to look in on a few ongoing WCS gorilla conservation projects. Then it's time to vote: Which one of the gorillas' habitats would you like to direct your admission donation to help save? Already you are doing something; you have made a decision and have become involved in saving wild lives.

Though Conway's concerns kept him firmly rooted at home—educating and inspiring zoo-goers, improving the animals' captive environments, and developing better breeding methods—he never forgot that the Bronx Zoo's primary mission was, and will always be, to preserve wild animals and their habitats all over the planet.

If Conway has his way, the zoos of the future will not be living museums where people come to observe wild animals in model ecosystems,

Visitors choose where to direct their admission donation.

72

when those wild homes have been all but eliminated. Never again can a zoo consider itself as merely a place to show animals. Instead, he has declared, "The future of zoos is to become conservation parks." A true conservation park would be a sanctuary for rare animals, a place that breeds endangered species and engages in outreach programs for saving wild habitats. All worthwhile zoos of the future, he believes, will take an active role in preserving species as well as habitats. Conway has been a leader in helping to convince all the world's zoos to strive for that goal.

As the Bronx Zoo's second century gets under way, the people of the WCS, as well as the directors of the best zoos around the world, agree—in the twenty-first century, all zookeepers must concern themselves with the same difficult questions: Will there be *any* wild places left on Earth by the end of this century? Will the "wild" animals of the future be bred only in zoo-run facilities? Even worse, will they be conceived only in test tubes, grown only in labs, raised only in zoos, never having seen anything resembling their natural environments? Will zoos be the last haven for wild animals? The people at the Bronx Zoo and the WCS are working hard to make sure they are not. The world's new heroes are spread out around the globe, in zoos as well as in the field, working with people of nearly every nation, helping them preserve their wild spaces so wild animals and human beings can live and flourish together long into the future.

Wildlife conservation demands a global ethic, in which wildlife and wild places are fundamental to life on Earth, not exotic destinations or aesthetic adornments. The Wildlife Conservation Society can inspire such an ethic through our living collection of wild animals. Through continued exploration, research and long term involvement in living landscapes, we can . . . discover pathways to sustainability, in which humans and nature can live together. To succeed in this effort is the conservation quest of the 21st century.
—Steven Sanderson, WCS president,
"The Second Century"

Wildlife Conservation Society researcher Dr. Amy Vedder with mountain gorillas.

Tagging a baby hartebeest, an African antelope.

A newly tagged gazelle calf.

Examining an elephant.

George Schaller on a gorilla study, Virunga Volcanoes.

George Schaller at work in China.

A keeper holds a chinchilla.

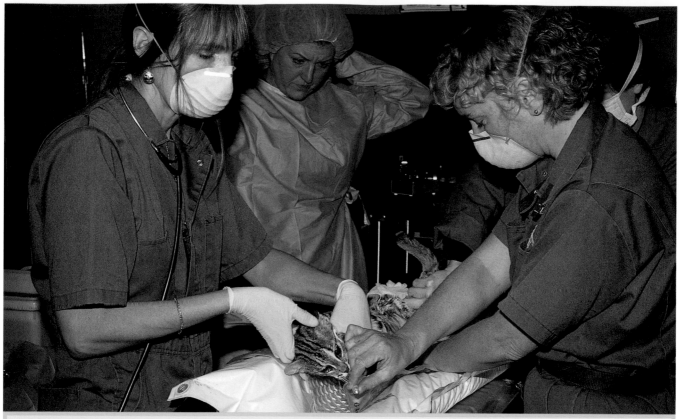

A leopard cat undergoes artificial insemination.

Capturing an anaconda.

A turtle hatchling.

BIBLIOGRAPHY

(Suggested books for further reading are bulleted.)

Baratay, Eric, and Elisabeth Hardouin-Fugier. *Zoo: A History of Zoological Gardens in the West.* London: Reaktion Books, 2002.

• Beebe, William. *Adventuring with Beebe.* Boston: Little, Brown & Co., 1955.

———. *Galápagos: World's End.* New York: G. P. Putnam's Sons, 1924.

———. *Jungle Days.* New York: G. P. Putnam's Sons, 1925.

• ———. *Pheasant Jungles.* New York: G. P. Putnam's Sons, 1927.

Bendiner, Robert. *The Fall of the Wild, the Rise of the Zoo.* New York: E. P. Dutton, 1981.

Blair, W. Reid. *In the Zoo: Representing Twenty-Seven Years of Observation and Study of the Animals in the New York Zoological Park.* New York: Scribner's, 1929.

Bouse, Derek. *Wildlife Films.* Philadelphia: University of Pennsylvania Press, 2000.

Bridges, William. *Big Zoo.* New York: Viking Press, 1941.

———. *Gathering of Animals: An Unconventional History of the New York Zoological Society.* New York: Harper & Row, 1974.

Crandall, Lee S. *A Zoo Man's Notebook.* Chicago: University of Chicago Press, 1966.

Croke, Vicki. *The Modern Ark: The Story of Zoos: Past, Present, and Future.* New York: Scribner's, 1997.

Dary, David A. *The Buffalo Book: The Full Saga of the American Animal.* Chicago: Swallow Press, 1974.

• Ditmars, Raymond L. *The Making of a Scientist.* New York: Macmillan, 1937.

———. *Strange Animals I Have Known.* New York: Brewer, Warren & Putnam, 1931.

• ———. *Thrills of a Naturalist's Quest.* New York: Macmillan, 1932.

Dolph, James Andrew. "Bringing Wildlife to Millions: William Temple Hornaday, the Early Years, 1854–96." Biography (Ph.D. dissertation held in the Zoo's library).

Garner, R. L. *Gorillas and Chimpanzees.* London: Osgood, McIlvaine, 1896.

Garretson, Martin S. *The American Bison: The Story of Its Extermination as a Wild Species and Its Restoration Under Federal Protection.* New York: New York Zoological Society, 1938.

Gould, Carol Grant. *The Remarkable Life of William Beebe.* Washington, D.C.: Island Press, 2004.

Hancocks, David. *A Different Nature: The Paradoxical World of Zoos and Their Uncertain Future.* Berkeley: University of California Press, 2001.

Hoage, R. J., and William A. Deiss, eds. *New Worlds, New Animals: From Menagerie to Zoological Park in the Nineteenth Century.* Baltimore: Johns Hopkins University Press, 1996.

Homberger, Eric. *The Historical Atlas of New York City.* New York: Holt, 1994.

Hornaday, William T. *The Extermination of the American Bison.* Washington, D.C.: Smithsonian Institution Press, 2002.

• ———. *The Minds and Manners of Wild Animals.* New York: Scribner's, 1922.

• ———. *Our Vanishing Wild Life: Its Extermination and Preservation.* New York: New York Zoological Society, 1913.

———. *Popular Official Guide to the New York Zoological Park.* New York: New York Zoological Society, 1899.

———. *Thirty Years War for Wild Life.* New York: Scribner's, 1931.

———. *Wild Animal Interviews.* New York: Scribner's, 1928.

International Cosmos Prize, 1996. Osaka: The Commemorative Foundation for the International Garden and Greenery Exposition, 1997.

Kisting, Vernon N., Jr., ed. *Zoo and Aquarium History: Ancient Animal Collections to Zoological Gardens.* Boca Raton: CRC Press, 2001.

Koebner, Linda. *Zoo Book: The Evolution of Wildlife Conservation Centers.* New York: Forge, 1994.

Livingston, Bernard. *Zoo: Animals, People, Places.* New York: Arbor House, 1974.

Malamud, Randy. *Reading Zoos: Representations of Animals and Captivity.* New York: New York University Press, 1998.

Margodt, Koen. *The Welfare Ark: Suggestions for a Renewed Policy for Zoos.* Brussels: VUB University Press, 2001.

• Martini, Helen. *My Zoo Family.* New York: Harper, 1955.

Matthiessen, Peter. *Wildlife in America.* New York: Viking, 1987.

McKenna, Virginia, et al. *Beyond the Bars: The Zoo Dilemma.* Thorsons, 1987.

Mitman, Gregg. *Reel Nature: America's Romance with Wildlife on Film.* Cambridge: Harvard University Press, 1999.

New York Zoological Society. Annual Reports, 1896–1900.

• Nichols, Michael, William Conway, et al. *Keepers of the Kingdom: The New American Zoo.* New York: Thomasson-Grant & Howell, 1995.

Norton, Bryan G., et al., eds. *Ethics on the Ark: Zoos, Animal Welfare, and Wildlife Conservation.* Washington, D.C.: Smithsonian Books, 1995.

• Osborn, Fairfield. *Our Plundered Planet.* Boston: Little, Brown & Co., 1948.

Page, Jake. *Zoo: The Modern Ark.* New York: Facts on File, 1990.

River and Plains Society. *The Vanishing West: Hornaday's Buffalo: The Last of the Wild Herds.* Fort Benton, MT: River and Plains Society, 1992.

Rothfels, Nigel. *Savages and Beasts: The Birth of the Modern Zoo.* Baltimore: Johns Hopkins University Press, 2002.

Sanderson, Steven, et al., eds. *Parks in Peril: People, Politics, and Protected Areas.* Washington, D.C.: Island Press, 1998.

Schaller, George B. *Golden Shadows, Flying Hooves.* New York: Knopf, 1973.

———. *Gorilla: Struggle for Survival in the Virungas.* New York: Farrar, Straus and Giroux, 1989.

• ———. *The Last Panda.* Chicago: University of Chicago Press, 1993.

———. *The Mountain Gorilla: Ecology and Behavior.* Chicago: University of Chicago Press, 1963.

———. *Serengeti: A Kingdom of Predators.* New York: Knopf, 1972.

• ———. *The Serengeti Lion: A Study of Predator-Prey Relations.* Chicago: University of Chicago Press, 1972.

———. *Stones of Silence: Journeys in the Himalaya.* New York: Viking, 1980.

———. *Tibet's Hidden Wilderness: Wildlife and Nomads of the Chang Tang Reserve.* New York: Abrams, 1997.

• ———. *The Year of the Gorilla.* Chicago: University of Chicago Press, 1964.

Still, Bayrd. *Mirror for Gotham.* New York: Fordham University Press, 1994.

Tobias, Michael. *Nature's Keepers: On the Front Lines of the Fight to Save Wildlife in America.* New York: Wiley, 1998.

Tudge, Colin. *Last Animals at the Zoo: How Mass Extinction Can Be Stopped.* Washington, D.C.: Island Press, 1992.

Welker, Robert Henry. *Natural Man: The Life of William Beebe.* Bloomington: Indiana University Press, 1975.

Wildlife Conservation Society. Annual Reports, 2000–2002.

———. *Saving Wildlife: A Century of Conservation.* New York: Abrams, 1995.

Wolfe, Art. *The Living Wild.* Seattle: Wildlands Press, 2000.

Zuckerman, Lord S., ed. *Great Zoos of the World: Their Origins and Significance.* Boulder: Westview Press, 1980.

Children's Books

Altman, Joyce. *Dear Bronx Zoo.* New York: Simon & Schuster, 1990.

Buchenholz, Bruce. *Doctor in the Zoo.* New York: Studio, 1974.

Curtis, Patricia. *Animals and the New Zoos.* Lodestar, 1991.

Halmi, Robert. *Zoos of the World.* Four Winds, 1975.

Johnston, Ginny, and Judy Cutchins. *Windows on Wildlife.* New York: Morrow, 1990.

Nirgiotis, Theodore, and Nicholas Nirgiotis. *No More Dodos: How Zoos Help Endangered Wildlife.* Minneapolis: Lerner, 1996.

Ricciuti, Edward R. *A Pelican Swallowed My Head.* New York: Simon & Schuster, 2002.

• Scott, Jack Denton. *City of Birds and Beasts: Behind the Scenes at the Bronx Zoo.* New York: G. P. Putnam's Sons, 1978.

Thomson, Peggy. *Keepers and Creatures at the National Zoo.* New York: T. Y. Crowell, 1988.

Yancey, Diane. *Zoos.* Lucent, 1994.

Articles

Beebe, William. "The Ecology of the Hoatzin," *Zoologica* 1, 1909, 45–66.

Warren, Adrian. "Relic of Prehistory?" *Wildlife,* October 1977, 447–495.

Zahler, Peter. "Crazy Like a Hoatzin," *International Wildlife*, July/August 1997.

From the Bronx Zoo Archives

Biographical folder of Fairfield Osborn

Biographical folder of George B. Schaller

INDEX

A heartfelt thanks to Nancy Siscoe for brainstorming this project and getting it under way. Thanks also to editor Michelle Frey and designer Kate Gartner for putting it all together so brilliantly and to Alison Kolani, Artie Bennett, and Donald Nekrosius for that extra attention to detail. We're especially grateful to all those at the Wildlife Conservation Society who provided expert help, including Diane Shapiro, manager of Photo Services; Suzanne Bolduc, assistant manager of Photo Services; Steve Johnson, manager of the Bronx Zoo Library; and Julia Mair, vice president, Television and Media.

THIS IS A BORZOI BOOK PUBLISHED BY ALFRED A. KNOPF

Text copyright © 2006 by Kathleen Weidner Zoehfeld

All images copyright © Wildlife Conservation Society except as follows: p. 50: © Elyssa Kellerman/Wildlife Conservation Society; p. 58: © Wildlife Conservation Society/C. A. Rogus; p. 61 right: © Wildlife Conservation Society/D. DeMello; p. 75 bottom left & right: © W. B. Karesh/Wildlife Conservation Society; top right: © Wildlife Conservation Society/D. DeMello; p. 76 top left: © Kay Schaller/Wildlife Conservation Society

The Wildlife Conservation Society saves wildlife and wild lands. We do so through careful science, international conservation, education, and the management of the world's largest system of urban wildlife parks, led by the flagship Bronx Zoo. Together, these activities change individual attitudes toward nature and help people imagine wildlife and humans living in sustainable interaction on both a local and a global scale. WCS is committed to this work because we believe it essential to the integrity of life on Earth.

Additional picture credits:
p. 10: image copyright © Library of Congress; p. 14: image copyright © Overholser Historical Research Center, Fort Benton, Montana

www.randomhouse.com/kids

Library of Congress Cataloging-in-Publication Data
Zoehfeld, Kathleen Weidner.
Wild lives : a history of the people & animals of the Bronx Zoo / by Kathleen Weidner Zoehfeld.
p. cm.
Includes bibliographical references and index.
ISBN 0-375-80630-X (trade) — ISBN 0-375-90630-4 (lib. bdg.)
1. New York Zoological Park—History—Juvenile literature. I. Title.
QL76.5.U62N4893 2006
590.73747'275—dc22
2005018943

MANUFACTURED IN CHINA
March 2006
10 9 8 7 6 5 4 3 2 1
First Edition